Turkeys

ABDO
Publishing Company
A Buddy Book
by
Julie Murray

VISIT US AT
www.abdopub.com

Published by Buddy Books, an imprint of ABDO Publishing Company, 4940 Viking Drive, Suite 622, Edina, Minnesota 55435. Copyright © 2005 by Abdo Consulting Group, Inc. International copyrights reserved in all countries. No part of this book may be reproduced in any form without written permission from the publisher.

Printed in the United States.

Edited by: Christy DeVillier
Contributing Editors: Matt Ray, Michael P. Goecke
Graphic Design: Maria Hosley
Image Research: Deborah Coldiron
Photographs: Corbis, Corel, Mark Kostich, Photodisc

Library of Congress Cataloging-in-Publication Data

Murray, Julie, 1969-
   Turkeys/Julie Murray.
       p. cm. — (Animal kingdom. Set II)
   Includes bibliographical references and index.
   Contents: Turkeys — What they look like — What they eat — Where they live — Puffing up — Nesting — Baby chicks — A turkey's life — Turkeys through the years.
   ISBN 1-59197-337-6
       1. Turkeys—Juvenile literature. [1. Turkeys.] I. Title.

QL696.G27M87 2003
598.6'45—dc21

                                                      2002033001

Contents

Turkeys

Turkeys have lived in North America for thousands of years. American settlers hunted turkeys. American Indians were the first people to raise turkeys for food.

Turkey is a favorite food for many people today. Some people hunt wild turkeys and eat them. People can buy turkey meat at stores, too.

Turkeys are **poultry** animals. Poultry are birds that people raise for food. Other poultry animals are chickens, ducks, and geese.

Ducks (top), chickens (middle), and geese (bottom) are poultry animals.

What They Look Like

Farm turkeys may have white, black, brown, red, or green feathers. Most wild turkeys have reddish brown or gray feathers. Turkeys have no feathers on their neck and head.

Turkeys

Turkeys have a **wattle** that hangs at their throat. They have a **snood** that hangs above their beaks. Male turkeys, or toms, have spurs on their legs. Spurs are sharp spines.

Farm turkeys are heavier than wild turkeys. Many farm turkeys are too heavy to fly. Farm toms can weigh up to 40 pounds (18 kg). Female turkeys, or hens, are smaller and lighter.

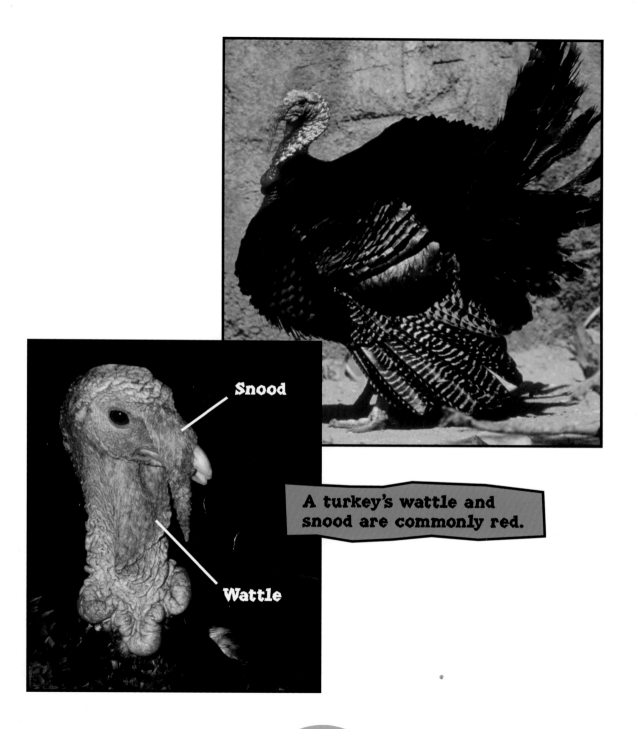

Snood

Wattle

A turkey's wattle and snood are commonly red.

Male turkeys are called toms.

Farm turkeys are often too heavy to fly.

Wild turkeys can fly and move faster than farm turkeys. Wild toms weigh between 10 and 16 pounds (5 and 7 kg).

Where They Live

Farm turkeys live in many places around the world. Wild turkeys live in the United States, Mexico, and Guatemala. They live in forests, fields, and near croplands. At night, wild turkeys fly into the trees to **roost**.

The colorful ocellated turkey
lives in Mexico and Guatemala.

Eating

Farm turkeys eat wheat, corn, and seeds. They also eat insects they find on the ground. Farmers give their turkeys clean water every day.

Many farmers feed their turkeys corn.

Wild turkeys spend much of their time searching for food. They often scratch the ground while searching. Wild turkeys eat insects, acorns, berries, and nuts.

Wild turkeys spend their day looking for food.

A Turkey's Life

Farmers take care of their turkeys. Some farmers let their turkeys run around outside. They stay inside a shed at night.

Some wild turkeys live together in **flocks**. Flocks look for food together. Some flocks only have toms. Other flocks only have hens and their young. Some turkey flocks have toms and hens.

Some farm turkeys spend the day outside.

Why Turkeys "Gobble"

Toms look for mates in late winter and early spring. They do special things to get a hen's attention. Toms puff out their body feathers and make "gobble" sounds. Toms will spread their tail feathers, too.

Poults

Hens lay between 10 and 15 eggs. A mother hen sits on her eggs to keep them warm. This is called **incubation**. Incubation helps the babies grow inside the eggs. They will hatch after about four weeks.

A young turkey

Baby turkeys are called **poults**. They have a special egg tooth. Poults use their egg tooth to break out of the egg. Newly hatched poults have soft down feathers. They can walk and eat right away.

After about two weeks, poults grow adult feathers. Poults that live on farms stay indoors. Farmers may let them go outside when they are six weeks old.

Important Words

flock a group of animals that live together.

incubation keeping eggs warm until they hatch.

poult a young turkey.

poultry birds that farmers raise for food.

roost to rest or sleep.

snood loose skin that hangs above a turkey's beak.

wattle the flap of skin that hangs at a turkey's throat.

Web Sites

To learn more about turkeys, visit ABDO Publishing Company on the World Wide Web. Web sites about turkeys are featured on our Book Links page. These links are routinely monitored and updated to provide the most current information available.

www.abdopub.com

Index